8 Things I Learned *from* Oprah

FROM A MANS PERSPECTIVE

By John H. Gregory

Copyright

The information in this book is intended to inspire, motivate and empower readers. It is in no way intended for diagnosis, prescribe or treat any health disorder whatsoever. The author and publisher are in no way liable for any misuse of the material.

All scripture quotations, unless otherwise indicated, are taken from the Holy Bible, King James Version (KJV).

ISBN 978-0-578-59410-1

Printed in the United States of America

A percentage of the Author's proceeds will go to the National African American Male Wellness Initiative

For more information:

Email: iampgregory@ausohio.com or acdunlap@ausohio.com

Dedication

First, I would like to acknowledge the Creator for birthing and endowing me with faith to trek upon this journey of awakening without faltering. During this sojourn, He revealed that I would share transformative life lessons from this sometimes painful and other times awkward expedition. It is through these experiences, as the great hymn of the Church, Amazing Grace declares, "...I'm found, was blind but NOW I see!" I know my life has indeed been blessed.

I would like to dedicate this book to my soulmate, the love of my life and wife, Pamela Gregory, whom I affectionately call PG. You are my loving partner in marriage, ministry and the marketplace—what a journey it has been. Your love and support has been endless and you are my source of inspiration and drive. Thank you for being my best friend.

≈≈≈

There is an ancient Chinese proverb that says, "*Love sought is good, but love unsought is better.*"

This book is the evidence of the unsought love moments that I have experienced in my life. It is my hope that you, the reader, will do the same.

Thank you

Thank you to my children, Francesco, DeVeonne, Perry, Crimson, Camden, Chaz and Tasha for your patience and sacrifice where you have had to share your dad with so many others. Thank you for supporting my dreams and being a part of my vision. Thank you for being who you are. Each of you in your unique way has allowed me to walk in my calling. As you travel through life remember not to define yourself by who others perceive you to be and try to make a difference in the world, no matter how small.

As your father, it evokes tremendous pride to witness how you have become fine young adults. I am truly blessed to have you as my children.

Acknowledgements

I wish to thank all the readers who embrace these words and implement these lessons in your life. My desire is that your lives will be changed forever, and that you will take what you have received and bless someone else.

Special thanks to Alicia C. Dunlap for providing me the human tools required to complete this project and guiding me through the process while capturing my words and transcribing my thoughts.

Pastor Macklin, I truly appreciate your editorial contributions of wordsmith and getting me to the finish line with this book.

My love and respect for my mother-in-law, Mother Shirley Shipp whose unconditional love and prayers are unmatched.

I am grateful for my dawg Chad, for patiently being my new set of eyes.

Finally, I am thankful for my amazing staff at The National Center for Urban Solutions, The Academy for Urban Scholars High School (Columbus/Youngstown), and The National African American Male Wellness Initiative. You have all played a part in some way or another.

Contents

Introduction 1

Chapter 1
It's Not the End of the World 11

Chapter 2
Let Yourself off The Hook 21

Chapter 3
Get Rid of the Noise 31

Chapter 4
Be Mad... But Talk to God Anyway 41

Chapter 5
The Power of "I AM" 51

Chapter 6
Gratitude 69

Chapter 7
This is Your Journey 85

Chapter 8
Go Tell Your Story 101

"Our words have creative power whenever we speak something, either good or bad; we give life to what we are saying." ***Joel Olsteen*** -

I Declare: **31 Promises to Speak Over Your Life**

Introduction

Walk with Me

"Mr. Gregory, you are a good man. You had a dream that nobody thought you would make happen. Not only did you do a good job, but you did it right." These were the words the judge spoke to me as I stood in the courtroom. After hearing these affirmations, I felt instant gratification as my heart regained its rhythm and a sigh of relief filled my soul. That instant, I knew I was not going to jail.

As I savored the moment, my excitement was short lived. Even though the judge had just given me his words of assurance and admiration, he was not done speaking. As he looked at me, putting his head in his hands, he said, "This is one of those days where I wish I had not come to work." "I have no choice but to sentence you to one year and one day in prison." Suddenly, I went from excitement to indifference. My world, as I knew it, was now obsolete.

While standing in the courtroom, so many things began to clutter my mind. How could I escape this moment? Where could I run? Was this the best I was going to get from my God? The God I served faithfully? The God I spent most of my adult life being obedient and saving other people? I wanted to disappear.

Whose Reality?

No matter how much good I had done, the reality that stood in front of me was evident, I was going to jail for obstruction of justice. Justice, the very principle I have spent my life upholding was now my enemy. I provided information to the grand jury believing the information was accurate. I spent my life advocating for the empowerment of people, helping to provide resources for employment, educating those in need, and helping our community become better, ironically I was facing jail time for obstructing justice.

I stood there awaiting this sentence and contemplating how to survive what I would be given. I began to think about how many storms have come and gone in my life, but this was the one storm I truly didn't think I was going to survive. There are times in all of our lives when one event takes us by total surprise. This was that time for me.

Memories of other people's storms flooded my mind and I realized I was not the only person who had storms and in the mist I also knew I was not alone.

I remember the day my friend James got a call that his son had been shot. According to authorities, the young man was lying in bed asleep and his best friend was in the next room playing with a gun. The gun went off, the bullet traveled through the wall and shot James' son in the head.

I also thought about parents who kissed their young children and sent them off to school only to receive a call that their children were being held hostage in a hostile situation at school. This is one of the places that children should be safe, but were not.

Thoughts of people who have encountered sudden heart attacks, strokes, unexpected deaths of beloved family members, or divorce, these moments, some more intense than others, each have a significant impact on the lives of all involved. Therefore, the emotions that overwhelm during these times seem unbearable. Some people respond with anger or a feeling of not wanting to go on living. The question of how to get out of the pain occurs and possibly convinces otherwise stable people that there is no reason to continue.

Prior to this moment in my life, I had never identified with these thoughts or emotions nor had I been faced with a situation that I could not control or repair. When my sister Iris died, I went to the doctors and told them to tell me the truth because I knew I could handle whatever they needed to tell me. This was the first death experienced my family endured, everyone was screaming and crying, falling out and they were completely distraught, I allowed my family to lean on me for comfort and guidance.

Even though my sister's death was one of the hardest things I had to deal with in my life, it did not compare to what I was feeling while standing in the courtroom of the Honorable Judge Gregory Frost, I felt vulnerable. Embarrassment, shame, fear and loneliness, were all felt simultaneously, all in a matter of minutes. I remember thinking, why did all of these people have to be in the courtroom? All I wanted was for someone to shake me and tell me this was a bad dream and that it would all be over.

Facing Reality

When I woke up the next morning I knew without a shadow of a doubt that my experience was not a dream. I sat up in my bed and thought, "What am I going to do?" I turned on the TV to just stare at something and then, I heard the voice of God say, for many years you have watched and listened to Oprah.

I had just started watching *Super Soul Sunday* with Oprah Winfrey and this was confirmation to continue and share her teachings with others who may not watch *Super Soul Sunday.* I remember when Oprah's *Super Soul Sunday* first aired; I convinced my partner and my entire office to tune in and watch. Although each Sunday she had different guests and addressed different topics, the episodes that stuck with me the most were the ones where people shared something they had overcome and the battles they had won in life by staying in the fight.

Many of the men who I worked with did not listen to her because they thought she was male bashing. However, I actually convinced all of the women in the office to listen to Super Soul Sunday. Oprah had a universal message of love and self-worth that impacted more than just women. Her audience for her original talk show was initially targeted towards females, but now she had *Super Soul Sunday*, which spoke to all people, and her delivery was inviting.

The guest she had on that Sunday talked about how people had to be broken to get to the other side of darkness. I was currently in a place of uncertainty, questioning how I was going to deal with going to prison for an entire year of my life. I didn't have time to spend in prison because I still had so much work to do for others. At that moment God spoke to me and said, "What have you learned from the many years of watching Oprah?"

This particular morning, I was sitting watching *Super Soul Sunday* as I had for the past month. As I listened, person after person kept speaking and the message was all the same, "It's not the end of the world. In fact, it's the beginning of where you are supposed to be." I heard it so clearly. I was being broken and my spirit was opening, so I could hear the instructions from God, he was telling me where he wanted me to direct my focus. In this moment, I realized the detailed message I was hearing was exclusively for me.

As I sat there on the bed, I began to reflect on the fact that I had been watching the Oprah Winfrey Show for years. Week after week I had exposed myself to these one hour sessions with Oprah.

It wasn't just about watching a TV show; I was learning lessons for my purpose in life. Her show introduced me to such people as Dr. Wayne Dyer, who talked about the power of intention and Deepak Chopra, who introduced

"I AM." As I began to think about what else I had learned from all those years of watching her show, the information flooded my head like a raging river.

As time went on, I could hear God speaking to my spirit. I heard him say the number '8' which represents resurrection and regeneration. I realized I needed to understand eight things. I stepped into this next portion of my life and shared it with the universe. Yes, it is true; when the student is ready the teacher will appear. I had been a student, and now was ready to share what I have learned throughout my life's journey.

Conclusion

As you read these pages, allow me to share with you my lessons and the journey my life has taken. Some of you may not be ready to read or embrace what you read on these pages, but if you keep reading over and over you will possibly hear God speaking to you saying, "You can make it! You can overcome the challenges of life! Hard times are not the end of the world! But most of all, you will win!"

As you continue to read, you will find the tools to move your life forward. You will learn that the experiences that you have encountered; the thing that you thought was the most difficult time in your life; will be the experience that leads you on a journey of discovery. A journey that will show you things about yourself that have made you stronger; given you more insight and equipped you with new tools to elevate you to where you ultimately want to be. You will learn that it really is in your moment of brokenness you identify your own power, the power that God has given you. You will learn that it's not the end of the world.

"And we know that all things work together for the good to them that love God, to them who are called according to his purpose." ***Romans 8:28 KJV***

Chapter One

It's Not the End of the World

This moment in my life was something I had never experienced before and no one understood what I was feeling, yet everyone had words to offer. While I knew people meant well, this was very painful for me. It's hard to hear anything while you are in the moment. People would come up to me and ask, "How do you feel?" In my head I would be thinking, how do I feel, the Judge just told me I was going to jail, the newspaper just reported that I was a thief, I have just gone from being the guy who helps people make a better life to a common thief. Really, how am I? The truth is that I was numb and didn't feel anything. No, let me correct that, I did feel something. I felt like I wanted to die!

This moment was one for me I would describe as overwhelming, a moment I will never forget. In fact, I know so many people who have had this type of moment and expressed feeling the same way. It's hard enough dealing with what has been presented before you, but it becomes even harder to accept when you think you are doing good for others or that you are a nice person treating everybody well, and people know they can depend on you but now, all of it seemed irrelevant.

My friend James is the nicest guy and spends a lot of his time working in the community helping young men determine alternate paths that bypasses jail. He has saved the lives of many young men within the community and dedicated his life to recognizing the good in people. So receiving the unimaginable call, that his son has been shot and killed by his son's best friend was devastating. These were two families who had been friends for years, spent time at each other's homes, and literally were considered family, but now life had dealt them a hand which brought darkness to a relationship that was once filled with light. Nothing I said at that moment in the days to follow made James feel better. I would call him often to check on him and he would just go through the motions. He couldn't see himself being able to go on, so he would lie on the couch day after day after day. I could see him slipping into a dark place and couldn't stand by and let this happen. So one day I went over to his house and said, "Enough is enough. Time to get up off the couch and come back to work." Reluctantly he came. He was not back at work in full force, but he had taken the first step.

I have learned over the course of my life emotions are a strong force. If allowed, emotions can consume every thought. You will try and figure it out, question what you did wrong and see it as punishment for past sins. Then there are the opinions of others. Such as the religious people who will suggest that you pray because God is trying to show you something at that moment. While they may have good intentions, they don't understand that you are angry at God. Questioning how the God you love could have let this happen to you. But it did happen to me. Just like the New Yorkers who went to work the day of 9/11, the unsuspecting parents of the children of Sandy Hook School Shooting or the mother who lost her baby after trying so hard to get pregnant. Perhaps you are my friend Tina who went for a check-up and found out that she had cancer and only a few months to live. We can always find stories that are worse than ours; but even that doesn't comfort us.

Confronting my own overwhelming moment, I heard all the voices and words from people, but I didn't want to hear about how others got through. I just wanted to know when this darkness was going to pass. I wanted to know if and when this would be over. I wanted this all to stop NOW! However, I had to stop, look around me and really embrace what was happening. This was not happening to me; it was happening for me. The truth will make you free, and the truth is that there are people who have been through much worse things than what I was experiencing, or even similar situations but they made it back. In fact, they came back even better.

James is a prime example of this very thing, he came back to work but he still had days he had to get through which were hard. Occasions such as the birthday of the son he lost, going to court proceedings, sitting as an observer through the trial of his son's killer, and then forgiving this same young man. This was not an easy task. I watched James month after month and each day he got stronger, just like the families of Sandy Hook and 9/11. They got stronger and resilient. Choosing not to be victims, they scheduled speaking engagements, organized events to promote awareness, and as hard as it might have been, were determined and resolved to keep moving forward despite the intense pain.

James, who has become an example to me, began to develop a new perspective. He worked for about a year, found a new job making even more money and went on to his new position with a new perspective on life. When his son got killed he thought it was the end of his own life. While it was devastatingly hard, James realized he could live. He grasped, like I had to realize, there is more to life than the moments that bring us pain.

This concept was my first lesson; I had to realize it was not the end of the world. I had watched it for many years on the Oprah show, people sharing their jaw dropping experiences. I would intently listen to them and always think, “Man these must be some of the bravest people I have ever heard.” Now it was my turn to tell my story.

The Lesson

What is the lesson I learned and how do I master these so others will know how to also master when the feeling of the end comes? There is still life left in all people? You must learn that life is fluid and it keeps moving regardless of what happens, so you must keep flowing with life. Whatever we encounter, understand this is just a moment in time. God sees one day as 1,000 years and more moments are coming. Anticipate them! They will be better. If you have lost a loved one you don't have to stop loving them, they still love you. If you made a mistake, God is a forgiving God and He throws mistakes into the sea of forgetfulness. There was nothing you could have done differently; it was already in the works before you came around.

The reality is, what you go through is not about you, so you have to let your ego go. The sooner you realize it's not about you, the quicker you will get back to you and your purpose. I can honestly say, it wasn't the end of the world at that moment, but it certainly felt like the whole world was against me. I discovered that there were plenty of people who were praying for me. In the Bible, Job thought it was the end of the world, he lost everything, but remember, life is fluid and Job got it back **DOUBLE!**

If you are facing a challenging situation in your life, I encourage you to hold on and don't give up. Things will get better, life will get better, just keep flowing with life.

Application

Write down one thing that you are being challenged with at this moment:

____

____

____

Now declare:

"This situation will not over take me! I will not give up! I am strong enough to handle what I am facing, and it is not the end of the world. I am more than a conqueror and no matter what, I will keep moving forward. I will not give up!"

Chapter Two

Let Yourself off The Hook

Forgiveness: *The action or process of forgiving or being forgiven (Webster)*

Forgiveness is a word that many people use, but many lack the true understanding of the importance of forgiving. While I have had my own personal experiences with forgiveness, it is a topic that has received a great deal of attention. It is actually more important than many human beings may realize. From magazine articles, to best-selling books, even the Bible teaches that we are to forgive those who have trespassed against. It is very important that you intentionally practice forgiveness, but is it really that easy?

Regardless of how simple or difficult this may be for some, it is important to put it into deliberate action. Not being able to forgive is one of those things that will keep you personally unable to move forward. As long as what should be released is retained we remain stagnated!

Two Sides to Every Coin

Many times forgiveness is examined from a single perspective, when in fact forgiveness has two sides, which are seeking and receiving. We seek forgiveness then it is received on our behalf.

Many people may feel like both sides of this coin can be a challenge to deal with and accept. I have learned that sometimes it is easier to forgive other people who have transgressed against you; however, it is not so easy to forgive yourself. When tragedy or things happen in your life, you spend a lot of time trying to figure out what you could have done to prevent the tragedy. It is at these times when many people fall into deep depression, holding themselves accountable for things that were simply beyond their control.

When my friend James' son was killed, he was depressed and isolated, trying to figure out what he could have done otherwise as a father. He would constantly question, like many of us do, his steps, his actions, his motive and lifestyle to make a determination if any of those things might have changed the situation. In reality there was nothing different James could have done to change the situation, it was out of his control.

Evaluate it

I am a believer that many times people hold on to their initial reaction and allow this to be the go-to feeling, emotion or thought that guides them through difficult situations. Although feelings and emotions are real, in some cases, you have to take time and evaluate the situation that you are facing. Where does the responsibility really belong? Could I have affected or altered the outcome? In some cases, you do have responsibility if your actions created or caused something to happen, and in other cases, like James, you do not. Either way, it is important that you evaluate and determine when you truly need to take accountability.

If there is a case where you could have done something differently, or the responsibility of a situation falls in your lap, acknowledge it, deal with it and if forgiveness needs to take place with others, go make things right. When all this is done... forgive yourself. Yes, I said, forgive yourself.

Forgiving oneself is sometimes the hardest task, but vitally important, not just for you, but for those who love you as well. As long as you hold on to your guilt or your shame, you will not allow yourself to develop and grow. In fact, you will remain in a place that you were not meant to stay.

The Internal Battle

Often times, when situations occur, we battle internally with so many different emotions. Our mind is bombarded by a million and one "What if" questions. We take on ***Guilt*** because it makes us feel like we are paying for something that happened and we feel like we should pay for it forever. Or we feel ***Shame*** and allow it to maintain CONTROL of us because something happened. As I have stated before, we cannot change the past, whether the situation was within or outside of our control, but we can choose where to go from here. We cannot stay in a place where we remain immovable or allow situations to control us. To win this battle we must choose to eliminate the “stinking thinking” chatter as our approach to victory.

Don’t Let Guilt Control You

Guilt is a very powerful emotion, one that if you let it, will continue to have you paralyzed, incapable to see clearly and unable to see a new path. It will keep you bound by circumstances, long after other people have gone on with their lives. Guilt will hold you hostage! It will have you in a place where things have changed, but you have convinced yourself that you should be persecuted. You believe that is your way of taking responsibility for your actions. Here are a few questions for you to consider. Are you the first person to make a mistake? How long should you be persecuted for making a mistake? Who determines this factor? And what are the repercussions of your persecution?

Ask yourself, why do I feel guilty? If there is something that happened that is totally out of your control, then why would you make yourself feel guilty? You have to continue to talk to yourself and really place the facts on the line. For example, someone passed away and you were not physically there. Would your presence have made a difference? Would it have changed the outcome? This is a scenario that many people deal with quite frequently. While we all want to be in a certain place, the question is, would the outcome have changed? In some situations, you just have to accept that there are certain things beyond your control that have no explanation.

As I reflect over my own life, I am still seeking to answer questions that have no real answers. While I try not to ponder on this, I realize that holding onto something that I could not change only prolongs feelings of guilt or shame. So I declare that if you want to have a life filled with happiness, and peace, forgive yourself.

If there is something that you should take responsibility for, absolutely, by all means you should do that. However, do not give yourself a life term sentence. Accept full responsibility for actions you could have truly done something about, or embrace the reality that there was nothing you could have done to change the situation and *let yourself off the hook*.

Take the First Step

If you are someone who has been holding onto guilt, shame or something that you should have released, it's time to let it go. You have too long held on to something that has held you in a dark place where you should not live. In the Bible how many times did Jesus say that you should forgive a person daily? Seventy times seven, so you know He has forgiven you. If Jesus has forgiven you, it makes sense for you to forgive yourself.

If there are circumstances which have happened beyond your control, there is no need for you to be ashamed, embarrassed or isolated! Speak to yourself, *"I had nothing to do with this circumstance. It happened to me, for me to make me better. I am wiser, I am stronger, and today, I am free!"* Let's start today with forgiving ourselves. This may not be easy, but if you have done what I suggested above, you have already taken the first step and begun the process.

Affirmation:
Declare out of your mouth

"I had nothing to do with this circumstance. It happened to me, for me to make me better. I am wiser, I am stronger, and today, I am ***free****!"*

Stand up *straight* and realize who *you* are, that you *tower* over your circumstances.

Maya Angelou

Chapter Three

Get Rid of the Noise

What people think and say can have such a tremendous impact on how we react to things, especially when we have a "this is the end of the world" moment. So many voices; so many opinions; and so much noise that can hinder, we can't even hear ourselves think. If we are going to move forward, then we must learn to get rid of the noise in our lives. As long as the noise is present our hearing is impaired. We are easily distracted. It may be difficult to hear our inner thoughts! The noise can be so deafening we fail to hear the stillness to settle us!

This revelation is probably the first thing I started practicing when I began watching Oprah. Prior to this, I knew it was important to have quiet time, and seek a place where you could reflect and silence the noise. Watching her *Super Soul Sunday* segments on this topic helped me to fully embrace the importance of such deliberate action.

Often times we don't realize the magnitude of the noise that exists in our lives and the impact it is having. We don't recognize the exhausting toll some people may be thrusting upon us and the fact that those relationships may be the loudest noise in our lives. I can fully appreciate Maya Angelou's observation, "Some people come to kill you." While you may disagree or refute this statement, I have come to believe it is true.

I remember a journalist who followed me most of my career, exclusively covering numerous stories and making money off of my charitable actions. One night a friend called saying, "Your friend Ron is doing a story on you." I immediately called Ron and inquired. His response was, "I am a reporter." I responded, "Were you going to call me and get my side of the story? You just reported that I was going to jail for 20 years." He responded, "Well, I'm a reporter."

While I understand everyone has a job to do, this action, in particularly coming from him, came as a surprise. During this time most people who knew me were reaching out to encourage me, yet this guy who had professionally and personally benefited from my work chose to exploit my darkest moments.

It was challenging dealing with the journalist who had created a negative noise pattern in my life, however, I had the voices of others advocating for me; the self-appointed spokesmen who became those counteracting voices. I remember getting a call one day from one of them stating, "I don't care what other people say about you, I just know you were trying to teach me something and I thank you." Another brother called to say, "I just want to do a story on you so people will know your side of the story because everybody makes mistakes." What I realized at that time was that what Maya Angelou said is right in her reflection, they come to kill you, and these are the people you need to run from.

Coming from all areas

The reality of life is that the noise in our lives can and will come from all areas. Sometimes, even from the unexpected. One unexpected area of noise will come from Christian people, saying things like, "If you get right with God, He will forgive you," or "The reason why this is happening is because God is trying to show you something." While these people may call themselves trying to help, God does no evil, so run from these people too. Don't even allow them to pray for you. When people pray for you, prayer is supposed to be unified, but with this mindset, your prayers won't be for the same purpose. They will be praying for your deliverance while you just want peace.

Another place the noise will come from is your family in the name of encouragement. Through their desire to be positive, they are killing you with the words they speak. For example, saying such things as, "See, I told you not to let your child go on that trip." If your marriage goes bad, "I told you not to marry that man." Oftentimes your family means well with good intentions. However, because they have inside knowledge they believe, in error, that their information and understanding of you are sufficient enough to rush your healing process, but many times it is quite the contrary.

Then you have to look out for the people who feel sorry for you. They come by and keep reminding you that you are going to be OK, or say things like, “I know somebody who went through the same thing.” My brother, who is a doctor, once told me no two illnesses are the same. I believe this holds true with life circumstances, no two situations have the same outcome.

Take the parents who tragically lost their children to violent crimes, all have a different journey. There may be similarities within the journey, but there is something distinctly different about each. However, people will come with all kinds of suggestions and answers in an attempt to help. If this overwhelms you, then I am compelled to say, you must run from them as well. Just because these people are family doesn't mean you have to allow them to drag you into their world. Family is created not just by blood, but also through relationships.

Even with the best intentions, some family is just not good for you. If it is vexing or toxic, then you must let it go for your own well-being.

How do you get rid of the pain?

Getting rid of the noise may not be an easy process, but it is one that is necessary. In the midst of your journey, your process might actually add to your pain, but once the noise is gone you will be closer to your healing.

This leg of the journey is one that will cause you to encounter people, some who will drain your emotions and energy. You may ask, "How can people do this?" The quick answer - they are doing what they enjoy doing, their job. This is something you need to be conscious of at all times. These are people who you want to avoid and keep at arm's length! You need people who will bring you strength, genuinely encourage you and add value and worth to you.

I have two friends, Mary Lou and Sheila who were a great example of friends who bring me strength. They kept sending me words of light during my darkness. They reminded me of the good that was surrounding me. Even if I didn't want to see it, through their consistent words of encouragement I was able to recognize the good in my moments.

In order to get rid of the pain it is important that you only allow people who want to build you and have true faith in what God is doing. If you know someone who is going through, the words you speak are vital to their journey. Be the good cheerleader.

During the darkest times of my life it was Pam, my wife, who was a trooper, my number one cheerleader. I would go into any battle with her and my kids as a part of my team. They all had been trained well and now it was their time to exercise their faith and power. Yes, you need friends, but only the ones who can speak your language, war for you in the spirit and release the true power of prayer. Those are the ones who should be walking with you.

In addition to raising your consciousness when it comes to people, during this process this will also be the one time you will learn the power of 'NO.' When people begin to share negative things that don't agree with your spirit, you must speak up and not remain silent. It is actually okay to say "NO!" if the occasion warrants it without guilt. For some, saying no is an extremely hard task, but learning to exercise this action is critical to silencing the noise in your life.

Chapter Four

Be Mad ..... but Talk to God Anyway

As we live, we find that life is full of challenges and situations that are simply defined as, "life happens." The first thing that happens when we are challenged or something happens is we start with the question, "Why me?" We go through the whole performance, "I am a good person," "I have never done anything to anybody; "God doesn't love me," or "Why am I being punished?" Many thoughts that question the 'why' are the things that we seem to meditate on instead of meditating on a positive solution.

I have a friend named Mary Jenkins who I am pretty confident felt the same way. She lost her husband at 23 and then later in life found herself and her children homeless. After conquering these obstacles, she found out that she had breast cancer. When Mary got the news from her doctor, I know her first response was, "Why me, haven't I been through enough?" With our own human minds there is just so much we can handle and when things happen to us we wonder, "Is this the end of the journey?"

Having emotions that make us question our circumstances is something that is very real. When Mary went through her situation I asked her, "How did you get past your test?" Her response was like so many others, "I talked to God." I said, "Come on Mary, you talked to God?"

When I first met Mary she was living in a homeless shelter with her three children. Later, she came to work for me, but she had a vision. She knew that while the journey she traveled was hard, it would prepare and allow her to start her own organization. Then one day she got the awful news that she had breast cancer. At that moment, it sounded like it was the end of her world, but Mary had received some great training. She tried to talk to people who had been through this before, but even their answers could not give her the comfort she was looking for. Mary gave up searching for answers and she began talking to God. Like Mary, many of us use our natural logic to figure things out when something big happens to us. We start trying to answer our own questions like, "What did I do?" "If only I had done something differently." There is nothing you can do to avoid what is going to happen on your journey. The only thing you can do is talk to God, listen and wait for the answer.

I consider myself to be a pretty smart person. For most of my life I have been able to figure things out; look at a situation and assess how it should be handled. Referred to as the "The Solutions Man," I could usually find the answer. However, this new journey that I encountered had me stunned, paralyzed and out of breath. Everyone I talked to made me mad. I couldn't understand why God would let this happen to me.

One day while having a, "I am mad at you session with God," I started talking to Him and really pouring myself out. I called myself really letting God have it. I talked about being abused as a child, being born out of wedlock and how disappointed I was with my life, yet I dedicated my life to Him. I felt like He just allowed stuff to happen to me.

Although I was in vent mode, God let me get it all out. In fact, I think He wanted to hear it all. He tells us to cast our cares on him, because He cares for us and that is just what I did, I unloaded. After I cast my cares on Him, I shifted from representing just myself to representing the rest of the world. Telling God about His business and how unfair this world was to people who walked with Him and all the suffering we had to endure. At some point I had nothing else to say. Yep, I got God told! I wanted to have this conversation with Him for a long time and now it was here.

Time to Listen

After I dumped all of my garbage I got silent, there was nothing else for me to say. Over the next couple of weeks, I started to hear God speaking to me. I remember saying, "God, okay, I'm listening. I will be quiet so you can speak. I need you to talk to me because I need answers." His first response was, "This, my friend, is a journey. I allowed you to travel it because you could handle it. The journey is not over so why are you throwing in the towel?

What is happening now is just a moment in time; it is not the end of your time."

Many times we tend to see life through rose colored glasses, but God's vision is clear. God went on to say, "You have been chosen to teach others to be awakened to My Presence and how would you know it's true if you had not walked this journey?" How would we know that God is real if we did not have experiences that break us or experience His healing power? We would not!

God continued to speak to me, "Nothing happens **to** you, it happens **for** you." As I listened, I heard very clearly what God was saying, but I still had questions. How could what I was going through be for me? I remember thinking, with all the kind words that had been spoken to me, all the people who released knowledge, how much I had blessed their lives, I had never heard those kinds of words.

Impactful does not even begin to describe what I felt at that moment. While I didn't know the answers to a lot of the questions posed, I knew at that moment, and I could truly comprehend that I had been chosen by God. I recognized just how blessed I actually was through my crisis.

Although I was facing a challenging time in my life I was nevertheless chosen by God! Now I could understand and embrace what I had heard so many times before. My mind goes to the Buddha proverb, "When the student is ready the teacher will show up." I was now ready and the teacher indeed showed up.

Shift in Perspective

As I continued to listen to God I was comforted with knowing He had been talking to me all along the way. However, in the midst of my challenge I was in so much pain because I could only see that moment.

In Mary's journey she was able to see her purpose and understood that she was to start *Christians Overcoming Cancer*, an organization that would understand all sides of a person's journey as they go through the loss of a spouse or someone needing food or shelter. Mary had walked a journey and now she could be the voice of God to many through her experience.

Talk to Him

As you go through your moment of hell, and understand that in life there will be a moment like this, you must do what is necessary to get out of it. You must first start by talking to God. This is critical and one of the most important actions you will take in life, talk to God. However, you choose; praying, crying, yelling, standing up or walking, just talk to Him. He won't judge you; He wants you to come to Him. When you come, open yourself up to listen. He will bring you the answers you are seeking. You might find the answer in a song, a person or through talking to someone else. When you hear it, you will realize the message **IS** for you. Don't look at whom, or question how, just know He will give you the answer.

Chapter 5

The Power of "I Am"

Death and life are in the power of the tongue: **Proverbs 18:21**

Words are singularly the most powerful force available to humanity and one of the most dominant forces in a person's life. Words can break, words can build, words can create and words can frame. The power of a word is life changing.

Throughout history there are different phrases that we hear that have framed the direction of a generation; phrases that ring from the lips of people, from the most famous to those in your local neighborhoods. Joel Osteen, Oprah Winfrey, Deepak Chopra, Steve Jobs, Dr. Wayne Dyer and so many others utilize a phrase that is not only transforming their lives, but everyone who attaches themselves to it, the power of I AM.

The truth of the matter is this is one lesson that I have adopted and believe in, the power of the words "I AM." As a prominent speaker, I have spent years encouraging and inspiring audiences through my words. The power within those two words, if fully embraced cannot only change a moment in time for a person, but change the very direction of their future. It is the declaration to one's self that not only speaks to their lives but empowers them to be confident in who they are. The power of "I AM" not only releases a declaration, but allows people to choose what they call in and out of their lives. What have you declared lately?

The truth is...

When looking at life, sometimes it is hard to focus on beyond what we see. Often, we spend a lot of time on things that impact us beyond our moment. We allow life's circumstances to weigh us down without realizing how heavy the load has become, simply because of our focus. Don't get me wrong, life happens, but you have the power to control the words that come out of your mouth. If you spend a lot of your life focused on staying depressed, continually declaring such things as "I AM" defeated, "I AM" unsuccessful, "I AM" hurt or any of these "I AM's" that are contrary to allowing you to become victorious over your situation, these things will find their way through people, circumstances and interactions to continue to stay in your life.

The truth is, whatever you say behind, I AM, opens the door for something to find you. I am a firm believer that life and death lay in the power of the tongue. That is why it is important for you to start affirming your life in the positive. If you are already doing this, that is great. But what words have you released recently into the universe that will take you beyond where you currently are? What words have you spoken that will challenge your situation and push your life in a positive direction?

It is easy in the good times to say positive affirmations, but what about when you are challenged and life gets hard and heavy?

For most people, it is in those times that the words don't come so easily. Moments when you are caught off guard and encounter things you never saw coming. I have had many of those moments throughout my life; my battles with cancer, losing my eyesight and learning to function in my new reality. The words out of my mouth became a critical piece for my life's journey. What I chose to say, what I elected to declare, what I proclaimed for my life became defining moments for me. I believe that when we encounter moments like this in time the universe is allowing us to enter into a new dimension of life through our words.

I want to share with you an experience I had with one of my friends, let's call her Tonya. Tonya was a professional, highly educated, nice woman whom I had known for quite a while. My family and I would spend time with her on numerous occasions and often held varied topics of conversations. While Tonya had a lot of things going for her in a positive manner in her life, many times her conversation carried more of a negative connotation.

One afternoon, after indulging in a conversation with Tonya, I squarely looked at her and said "Tonya quit speaking to the negative and start declaring what you want to be." Tonya encountered many challenges in her life. She had recently come through a health battle, finalized a divorce, and was in a place that she never thought she would be.

Her reflection: When Tonya looked at her life's mirror, the reflection cast was of a middle aged woman with a master's degree, a prominent successful position and wife to a wonderful man who was an FBI agent. She had what she viewed as the middle class American dream family. Then suddenly one day everything changed. What once was a space of security, had now become a fragmented life that she no longer recognized. So Tonya could not look at life the same way, but had to see it differently. As long as she confessed what she was not, her life continued to spiral in a direction that she did not intend to go. There had to be a point where she relinquished where she was and acknowledged where she wanted to be. At this moment Tonya was broken, but she could be healed.

As Tonya and I talked over lunch, I spoke with her about her confession and convinced her that if she confessed out of her mouth, “I am great, I am a strong woman, and I can survive and fulfill my purpose,” the universe would begin to line up and wherever success was it would begin to find her. Through her words she would begin to experience her new universe.

Over the next several months, Tonya began to practice the positive “I AMs.” Her first encounter with the positive “I AM” came when she obtained her dream job. She had always wanted to work in Human Resources but kept running into roadblocks. As she declared to herself and over herself, she finally got the position she always wanted. Her next “I AM” came as she received an opportunity to move to another city, another desire that had not been manifested, until now.

Today when I see Tonya, she is not the same person as before. Life has drastically changed and the perspective along with it. She no longer allows her present circumstances to dictate what she declares over her life. She confesses, “I AM exactly where I want to be and

I am no longer in the world of defeat or depression." She is living in her world of "I AM" successful.

Many people fail to understand that the power of their own confession is the thing that keeps them in the place where they are not achieving what they desire. It is a place where they may feel safe, but actually hinders them from moving forward in success. I have a friend who started a business and from the very beginning began to practice the declaration process of "I AM." He didn't know where he was going to end up, but one of his declarations became, "I AM" successful. Today he is a successful developer of a million-dollar business. While he may not have recognized it at the time, life was teaching him lessons throughout his process. If we watch and pay attention, we will see that lessons are being released daily on our journey, and if embraced in the right way, these same lessons will empower us to move past broken states into a blessed state.

Releasing the Words:

Merriam-Webster defines **Word** *as a sound or combination of sounds that has a meaning and is spoken or written: something that a person says: An order or command.*

Many people ask the question, do the words we speak really have weight? Do they really transform, create or cause things to come into fruition? Absolutely! According to this definition, words command and bring order.

What are you releasing out of your mouth? What has been your declaration? What are you placing after the words, "I AM?" This small, but powerful phrase has become a connecting factor of order that allows you to put out in the universe the things that will begin to shape and define you as a person. Through tragedy, a break up, a death and some unbelievable life circumstances, the declaration of how you identify, your "I AM" will be your stand or break moment.

When I was faced with dealing with cancer, I had to make a choice of what I would declare. Would I succumb to the circumstances, or would I declare that I would live and not die? My declaration became "I AM" strong, "I AM" healed, "I AM" not done with my life's journey, "I AM" going to finish the purpose that I was placed here for.

We are all faced with these moments. You might be in the midst of one of these moments right now. Are you facing an illness or sickness? Start declaring out of your mouth, "I AM healed." Allow whatever healing is to start finding its way to you. I know that you are thinking, how is just verbalizing bringing healing? Life is a process, and everything we encounter has one. Vocalizing that you are healed is the beginning process of becoming healed. Whether it is physically, mentally, or spiritually, the process begins with opening your mouth. The release of the words changes the thinking in your mind. There is a direct correlation between the two.

My Declaration

I have learned over time that the power of my words not only shapes my world, but helps to order my thoughts so that my actions fall into alignment with my words. Why is this important? In order for things to manifest, everything has to be in alignment. What I think, what I say, and then my actions will follow. We act or react to what we believe.

Every morning I arise; I have a routine which includes me making personal declarations to myself. I have my own series of "I AM" statements, including saying to myself that I AM loved. These three simple words have not only affirmed my life, but helped me to love others in a greater capacity because I understand the concept of love. Being able to utter these words, I AM loved starts a process, as we said earlier, that calls forth this action in your life. The declaration begins to send all the things in your life that love you directly in your direction. In fact, what you will find is that whenever you need love, love will come to you, again because you released what you are and what you needed into the universe.

Of all of our emotions, I believe love is the most powerful thing that we have because the premise of love came from a source which I believe is the foundation of truth, God's Word. God said that the greatest gift that you can give is love, and that is who He is, Love.

So these three things continue forever [endure; remain]: faith, hope, and love. And the greatest of these is love. (I Corinthians 13:13)

Love-*An intense feeling or deep affection*

Webster

What is your Declaration?

Asking one's self can be a challenging moment because sometimes we don't know what to say. We don't know where to start. Let me help you. My advice is that whatever you feel is that thing which wants to shape your personality, speak life into your situation, or frame the next part of your life, put it in writing (*write the vision and make it plain*). Take some sticky notes and write down positive affirmations for your life that align with your desires. Then take those same sticky notes and place them strategically in areas such as your bathroom or places and spaces that you frequent and which will force you to look directly at them. Why is this important?

When I get up in the morning the first thing that I say to myself is that I AM a winner! And I believe the words that I am speaking. My life has not always been easy, but I have decided that no matter what happens in life, I am winning. So I declare that into the universe daily, I declare it to myself, and out go out into the world and win!

What I am sharing with you may not be easy for everyone, however, I am not telling you to do anything that I don't apply to my own life. My day starts out with me setting the pace and tone in how I will respond to the universe that day. When adverse things come my way, I just look at those things and remind myself that "I AM" a winner. The trial may come, but it will not overtake me. I am a conqueror and can overcome anything that life throws my way. Is it easy, NO! Does it take perseverance? YES, but "I AM a WINNER!" no matter what.

It is important that you truly believe what you declare over your life because there will be moments where this will be challenged by people. Everyone may not agree with your "I AM" statements, but that is not for them to believe, it is your journey, your declarations and your life. When someone comes to me who may not agree, I don't get mad, argumentative or combative, I simply go into my "I AM" bag and pull out, my I AMs, I AM loved, I AM blessed and I Am a Winner. These simple, yet powerful words diminish the negative experiences because I have defined who I am.

I teach a class and in the class I instruct the participants to identify 5 -10 people who are distractors in their lives. I direct them to call them using this script, "Hello, this is (insert your name) and I'm a winner" and hang up! While this may seem silly to some, it is in fact an empowering action that causes unbelievable change in relationships and how people are viewed. Simply letting people know that you are defining YOURSELF as a winner changes the game in your favor.

So change the game! Define yourself and let the world know that you are a winner. I can tell you from my own experience of waking up and finding myself in an unfamiliar place, all that I went through being blind, my affirmation was the one thing that I know kept me seeing life in the positive and having blessings coming my way. When I realized it was not the end of the world, I began to say, I AM a winner, and really believed what I said. When all things came into alignment, I began to watch doors open, that I never thought would. I watched all kinds of positive opportunities come up for me. When many people thought it was over for me, the power of my words began to shape my universe for a greater success that I had yet to experience.

So when you find yourself in a place where you need encouragement, refine your existence by saying who you are:

I AM smart

I AM intelligent

I AM prosperous

I AM blessed

Whatever your end is to your "I AM," know and believe that what you say behind I AM, that's what you become.

Declare your I AM

I AM______________________________

I AM______________________________

I AM______________________________

I AM______________________________

I AM______________________________

I AM______________________________

I AM______________________________

I AM______________________________

"By faith you need to walk like a king, talk like a king, think like king, dress like a king, smile like a king. Don't go by what you see. Go by what you know. There is royalty in your DNA. You have the blood of a winner. You were created to reign in life." **Joel Olsteen** -

I Declare: **31 Promises to Speak Over Your Life**

Chapter 6
Gratitude

"In everything give thanks for this is the will of God in Christ Jesus concerning you". –

1 Thessalonians 5:18

Over the course of my life I have learned many lessons, sometimes the easy way, and sometimes the hard way, but the lessons have been learned. While they have been vast, one of the most important things that I feel I have learned is to be grateful. Showing gratitude is an important part of our journey.

This action is essential and if applied can contribute to the development and success of your life. Being grateful is not only for you, but is also about the seeds that are sown into the lives of others. Seeds, if planted correctly, will yield a harvest.

Our lives are based upon a connection of actions. I believe that many times people fail to realize that one thing is connected to another. We all desire to be successful, and there are definitely different pathways to success, but in all of our journeys, there are key principles that if aligned, will bring us to a positive result. Being grateful is one of those principles that I believe people fail to realize the importance of, when in fact, this is one of the most vital aspects of our life's journey.

Now I'm not talking about just being thankful because someone has been nice and kind, which is important, but I am talking about having a posture in life that you are always showing gratitude to the Creator for the things He has allowed you to be blessed to accomplish. I am ultimately talking about an attitude of gratitude.

As I have looked at people who have been extremely successful, spiritually, financially, etc., various characteristics stand out, but one common denominator in which I have found is derived from those who have left an impression on me by exhibiting true gratitude. Beyond their words, it has been the humility of their spirit which has shown their gratitude for life.

Many times when we think or hear of someone being grateful, verbal expressions are the first things that come to mind. When we hear a person say "thank you" or "I appreciate you" we associate this with gratitude. While this is a form of being thankful, I think sometimes people are challenged in knowing how to show gratitude.

The Bible tells us not only to show love in word, but also in deed. The action or deed reinforces what a person has verbally conveyed, and sometimes speaks more volume than actual words. I believe that it is through the action of gratitude that people not only know how individuals feel, but also allows people to see the love of God in a tangible way.

Validation is important! I believe everyone wants to receive love, as well as, feel affirmed and appreciated. So when things happen in our lives that are contrary to this, we question did we deserve it. The truth of the matter is, when we are blessed to have great finances, good health, and experience other positive things in our lives, we should recognize that it is a gift from the Creator. Every day will not be a good day, but simply having the breath of life makes it a blessed day. For this we should show our gratitude and be appreciative in our hearts.

Expressions of Gratitude

While we dialogue about showing gratitude, there are many ways to express appreciation. It can come in the form of words, gifts, and even the giving of your time. For example, you may find yourself having a great deal of time on your hands. Instead of doing nothing, or even something that benefits your personal needs, you may choose to volunteer your time. Consider visiting a school and reading to children at lunch time. Make yourself available to serve at a local food pantry or dining hall to feed the homeless. These are examples of showing gratitude and consequently the love of God through your actions. You were blessed with free time and used your time to bless others with patience and compassion.

Another example of showing love may be that you have a friend who is going through an illness, something that maybe you have experienced. They may need someone not only with compassion, but someone who knows the journey from a different perspective. You may be that person; the person who can not only sympathize, but empathize with their situation; even the need to ask for help. So you may be the one who can drive them to appointments, help them make sense of the unknown, offer to be a supportive listening ear and offer assistance or assurance, in whatever form that is needed for that moment. As you are grateful for your own life, it becomes easier to impart into and bless the lives of others.

Reflection

As I reflect on the journeys of my own life, through cancer, almost incarcerated, the impact these situations had on my family, and the many moments of decision I have encountered, I believe it was the gratitude of others that sometimes I didn't see which really got me through. I remember going to court, standing before the judge and hearing his words, "Mr. Gregory you're a good man, and I believe that you did which you thought was right. You had a dream no one thought you could do. Not only did you do a good job, but you did it right." I remember thinking that his words meant absolutely nothing. I reasoned that he was simply trying to find something to say, that is until I read a newspaper article dealing with that moment.

Not only were his words quoted, but it published comments by others who verbally gave their support and appreciation for me. Words from people who genuinely supported me for the work I was doing to transform lives in meaningful ways. I have always believed that the work I do is my calling, and is important to my community, but to know that others truly felt the same way blessed and strengthened me.

During that time, I received many text messages, phone calls and encouraging words even through social media. People shared that they knew what kind of person I truly was. Many in their own way reinforced that it was just a moment in time. It was a moment that was not a reflection of who I was as a person, but a moment that would give me stamina to endure while I continued walking through my journey.

As I think about how hard that time was in my life, I think about the strength I drew from the sincere gratitude of others. Individuals, who I knew personally, as well as those whose lives I didn't even know I had touched. Their words of encouragement, acts of kindness and for some, simply providing a listening ear to safely vent without judgement gave the support I needed. There was a time when I never had to ask for help, God would just send people to sow into my life. For example, there would be times when I would go to pay my bill at a restaurant and someone anonymously had already paid for it. On one occasion I had to address a situation, and someone had already insured that it was rectified.

Prior to that experience, I had a level of understanding of what gratitude was, I believe it was through this very public experience that I began to discover the actual power of gratitude. I believe their actions sealed their gratitude and gave me the grace and mercy to keep moving forward.

Showing Gratitude

Being on the receiving end of someone showing gratitude is a great feeling. One who encourages, affirms and at times empowers the recipient of this action.

While I have appreciated those moments of receiving encouragement through others actions, I believe it is equally as important to be the person showing acts of kindness. It would be amazing if everyone operated in a spirit of gratitude on a continual basis. Could you imagine the impact it would have on our community? It would be amazing.

Just as negative actions can affect or impact the life of a person, the action of gratitude can do the same. In fact, it has been said that when a person shows gratitude, the real significance of a person's ability of kindness gets exhibited. Have you shown gratitude to anyone lately? Have you experienced acts of kindness that have encouraged you to keep moving forward? Take a moment to deeply reflect on this.

The Challenge

While it is easy, so to speak, to appreciate and encourage individuals who show you acts of kindness, how do you respond to people who don't extend the same level of thoughtfulness to you? What about the person who abuses or misuses you or a loved one? Do you allow the actions or behaviors to negatively affect what you will do? While I understand mistreatment from others can adversely affect a person's responses or actions, the answer is a resounding, NO! It is not easy to treat people with kindness or even show gratitude when simply put; people are not nice to you.

However, I have learned not to allow the actions of others to dictate what I do, nor will I permit it to affect my life.

How do you deal with this? The Bible directs us to pray for those who despitefully use us. Forgive those as Christ has forgiven. This can be a hard task at times, but Jesus showed us this by example as he hung on the cross. He asked God to forgive them, the unthankful people who had gathered there screaming for Him to die. As He was being crucified for the sins and injustices of humanity, all the while He asked God for mercy on their behalf. While we are not the suffering Savior, we have an example of what to do when others fail us. As challenging as this is, this should be our actions as well.

Many times we try to figure out why people are not thankful. The truth is sometimes people don't realize what they are doing or the impact it will have on others. I know you are probably thinking, "People know what they are doing," but truly this is not always the case. We must remember that if we are chosen to have the knowledge of good and evil then we have been blessed to understand the difference between knowing and not knowing. In possessing that information we have to know that we should always show gratitude because of who we are created to be.

At times this truly is easier said than done. Sometimes it's difficult when going through hardships, such as losing a loved one, not getting a job or promotion you desire, going through a divorce or trying to fight a life threatening illness. Life circumstances are difficult, and showing gratitude in those times can be challenging. Trust me, I understand. At times I have found it to be so difficult to be thankful when going through things that I felt were so unfair to me. I would look around and think, there were so many other people who I felt should be going through what I was going through instead of me. I was not trying to judge others, but would look at what I was doing in my family, in my community and in other's lives and feel that it was so unfair.

Then one day I came to the realization that while things were not perfect I needed to change my perspective. I needed to change my way of thinking. I needed to start being thankful for the little things around me. Even though it was hard, I started being thankful for the situation. At the time, I was dealing with going blind. It was hard initially, but it became easier for me to really walk through this part of my journey because I realized that these issues were only temporary and came to teach me about my life's journey. As I changed my perspective and shifted my focus, I continued to declare words that aligned with where I wanted to be. I turned bitterness and anger into gratitude and thanksgiving.

Yes, you're probably thinking, gratitude for going blind? I will tell you that my gratitude about me being blind is about all the things I experienced during my blindness. I've learned a tremendous amount of things about myself. I have the resolve and strong ability to be resilient with the enabling of the Creator of the universe. I believe it is the gratitude that I have shown in this time of my life that has afforded me the opportunity to experience a true sense of what it means to walk in the spirit of God. I have been forced to walk as the Bible says, without sight, but in complete faith. If I wasn't blind right now would I be doing other things? Yes, but it's okay. I am in a good space and know that it is the posture of my heart of gratitude that has me here. My gratitude for these moments is so overwhelming that people often come up to me and want to feel pity for me or offer me encouraging words that are not reflective of where I am in my experience. They have not realized that the gratitude that I have developed through this journey has been a tremendous encouragement for me.

I encourage you to allow the spirit of gratitude to be an integral part of your daily life. It is powerful, yet an easy principle to comprehend. No matter what you face, the words you hear, or even the actions of others, regardless, you show gratitude. I promise you, it will change your life.

Application

Take a moment to think of several things you are thankful for. Write them down below:

____

____

____

____

____

____

____

Is there anyone you can bless or show an act of kindness to? List them, what you can do and make a date when you will do it.

____

____

____

____

____

____

____

____

Chapter 7

This Is Your Journey

At approximately 5 am, I woke up at my usual time and proceeded to follow my normal routine. I entered my bathroom, faced the huge mirror at home, looked into it and told myself "I AM GREAT"! This action is a very important part of my daily routine. Remember, the power of declaring to yourself, the "I AM" affirmation shifts and aligns things for the materialization of your words.

While my routine started off the same this morning I decided to lie back down and rest until 7 am. I went back to sleep and woke up several hours later. As I opened and wiped my eyes this time, I realized that my vision was blurred and cloudy. I really could not see clearly. Normally when I wipe my eyes my vision eventually comes into focus, but this day things were different. My vision was not becoming clearer; there was an extended delay in my focus.

I didn't know what was going on, however, I knew that something was not right. I told my wife that I needed to go to the doctor because I was having a hard time seeing from my right eye. I had experienced this same thing with my other eye. Six months prior I had gone blind in my left eye, and now I was facing, out of the blue, a similar episode, but now with my right eye.

My wife immediately made an appointment for me to be seen by the ophthalmologist. His prognosis was that my eyes looked dry. He recommended that I go see a specialist to address the issue. Although I had already gone blind in one eye, the doctor did not seem overly concerned or feel that the issue with my right eye would result in total blindness. However, he recommended that I see a specialist who could address the dryness in my eyes. Getting in to see the specialist was not an easy process. I'm not sure if it was level of importance, lacking the sense of urgency or simply the process of scheduling, but initially they could not get me in for two weeks. My wife, watching what I had already gone through, and aware of what I was presently going through, realized this was unacceptable. She called the office again and was able to get me an appointment within 24 hours. Pam is my greatest advocate and supporter!

Upon being evaluated by the surgeon, they decided that surgery would be the best option for my situation. They said they believed that all was well and were optimistic that my vision would once again become clear in my right eye; however, I never regained my sight after the surgery.

This was something that was mind blowing to me. One day I had my sight and the next it was gone. The doctors were confused as well. They said that as a result of the surgery my right eye was beautiful and no visible damage could be seen, yet they could not explain why now I suddenly could not see.

After the first surgery, I met with three additional specialists and endured another surgery, all with the hopes of regaining my vision. It was alarming for me to experience the loss of sight in my good eye suddenly, without warning or any signs that there was a problem. Yet here I was. The specialists, again three of them told my family that my eyes would be okay. They saw no reason why my sight would not be restored, yet three years passed and I never regained my sight.

Realizing my journey

Since this time I have seen numerous specialists, both locally and at the renowned Cleveland Clinic, all looking for answers to a question they have yet to answer. When I spent time at the Cleveland Clinic I remember the surgeon telling me, "Of all the tragedies in the world which does not make sense, you being blind is one of them."

As hard as that moment was for me, to encounter something that I never saw coming and am not even sure I was fully equipped for, I have come to realize that this is my journey.

I often say to people, if life has brought you lemons, yes you should make lemonade, because this is your journey. It is the hand that you have been dealt, because now the question becomes, what will you do with that hand? Will you take what is given to you and settle, or give up? It is always your choice! You can look at the hand you have been dealt and consider how to play to win. You can decide to take those same lemons and make lemonade.

Is this an easy task? Absolutely not! It did not come easily for me. There were many moments where I questioned my situation, and even the Creator, but I got to the point of realizing that I AM a winner and began to declare that to myself. Because I am a winner, I had to keep moving forward. I could not give up or relinquish my power. I had to keep moving forward. My journey was not and is not just about me, but about the legacy I am leaving for my children, my family and those who the creator has ordained me to touch. So as hard as it was, I had to make lemonade out of the lemons life had given me.

What has life thrown at you that you didn't see coming your way? What lemons have shaken your life and maybe even shattered you to the core? Has it been an incurable illness? Maybe being unjustly discharged or fired from a job. Or maybe you are that parent who lost a child to violence or some other tragic situation. Whatever it is, know that it is not the end of our journey, and while it may feel like it, it is not the end of the world. In fact, it is a moment that you may not understand, lacking clarity as to why it occurred, yet you are faced with it. So, I challenge you, at this moment, as hard as it may be, to accept that it is our journey, and KNOW that you can make it through.

You are stronger than you think

Many times we are faced with things in life that we feel will overtake us, and for some people that is the case, but that is not the desire of the Creator for your life. The desire is that you would thrive in the strength that you possess, which is greater than you realize, because you were chosen.

In the Bible it was recorded by the prophet Jeremiah that he was chosen before the foundation of the earth, as are you. You were chosen to win and this journey was chosen for you. The universe knew and understood that you could not only walk it, but walk it out. Contrary to what you may feel in the midst of your challenges, you can handle it. Here's living proof, YOU have been handling and readjusting to your situation all along! You have survived 100% of EVERY bad experience in your life to date! You possess a strength that is greater than what you think and it is cultivated through trials and lessons that are being taught on your journey. The lessons that you have learned or are learning, as you will see in my last chapter of this book, will empower you not only be strengthened individually, but enable you to share with others so that they may be strengthened as well.

While you may not realize it in these moments that may seem to deplete your strength, you are not walking this journey alone. You are not the first nor will you be the last to walk in this pathway. There are other people who are walking the same journey and need to hear a voice that says, "It's okay, you can make it;" a voice that not only speaks the words, but a voice that has lived the words.

Many times when we go through things, we try and look for the "whys" in the circumstance. Why is this happening to me? Why am I being punished? Why am I going through this? All of these questions are natural responses to frustrating circumstances, and sadly, we may never know the answer to any of the whys. But what we do know is that circumstances are not created out of revenge. You are not being punished because of the absence of God's love for you. In fact, it is the opposite. The universe knows that you were chosen for this journey; chosen to carry the cross. The truth is this journey really isn't about you. It's about what you are going to do with your experience, what you are to learn throughout your walk and what you apply to your life will impact others around you. The lessons of gratitude, endurance, longsuffering and love will be essential keys in helping to frame your view and perspective of the universe and your future.

It is very important to remember these key principles so that when life happens, and it will, and you encounter things that you cannot explain, you will remember this is not for your destruction, but ultimately for your strengthening. It is not necessarily a payback for anything in your life. If it is allowed, it is because the journey was created for you.

Reflection

For me, I have looked over my life many times and asked the question "why?" I felt as though life was unfair and questioned at times whether I could really walk out of this journey. While I have not always known the answers to those questions and cannot explain why I was chosen for this journey, the truth is, I know that I was, and it's okay.

For some people, asking the question "why" is a hard thing to do. They feel as though things will get worse or there will be a repercussion for inquiring about what they are facing. I have never been one who sat silently when there was a question to be asked. The Bible says that you have not because you ask not, and truthfully, how will you know if you do not ask.

I remember one-day sitting at home, thinking about everything surrounding my situation. Thinking about how my life had changed, and questioning how I got to this present state in my life. I knew I did not have the answers to the questions. I needed to know something that would not only sustain me, but help me to keep moving forward. When I asked the Creator the question, the answer that I got was simple, in fact maybe too simple. The Creator knew that I could walk this journey. I was stronger than I thought, wiser than I knew and more powerful than what I had experienced up to this point. The Creator knew I could walk this journey, and in that moment, I knew I could as well.

Every day on this journey is not easy, and there are definitely moments when I find myself very lonely and in the "I feel like no one understands" zone. Some days I battle with depression or contemplate, "should I take my life and end the journey?" Then there are days I'm overwhelmed with happiness and peace, and find the strength to keep moving on. Days where I remember that I AM strong, I AM a winner and I can make it through this journey.

I can honestly say that in spite of my moments of hesitancy, every day of the journey brings a new perspective of who I am as a person and my purpose. Daily I am afforded an opportunity to be able to touch someone else's life with the truth about their ability to get better in this universe. In spite of what we sometimes think, there is really no situation I believe that can overtake you. I know and understand that parts of the journey are hard to comprehend because we look at the reality in front of us, looking at what we can and cannot control. But despite the challenges you must have faith and fortitude to believe that you can make it.

Faith- *Complete trust or confidence in someone or something*. (Webster)

Despite my challenges in life and the questionable moments throughout my journey, faith for me is not a deficiency. I truly believe that good is all around me and that if I continually declare that out of my mouth then good will become visible and a tangible force in my life.

I encourage you to look beyond the moment, beyond the current circumstances and recognize that this is your journey and you were chosen for it. Is it easy? No. Will it take work? Absolutely. Are you walking it alone?

No. Can you walk it out all the way through? Yes.

Your walk may not be easy, but it is important to keep walking and moving forward. The truth is, it is hard to not allow moments to overtake us, but you must remember what in fact a moment is by definition: ***A very brief period of time.*** There will be moments of peace and happiness, and then harder moments of discouragement. But remember whatever moment you encounter will be connected to another moment, and another moment. Moments are not an eternity but they are brief. Yes, they are brief. While the impact may seem long, we must remember that they are just a *very brief period of time.*

With this in mind, I encourage you to walk your journey with pride. Hold your head up and walk through the doors that will open for you and close the doors that God shut behind you. Meet the new people you have been destined to encounter and let go of those who need to be released. Step off the shore line and explore the new places that will give you greater understanding, and leave those that are holding you back because there is a new world for you to see beyond the seashore.

You were created to be great, and going through your journey is a process to help cultivate your greatness. Take the words of the wise, one who has walked far in this journey, let go of the words of the fool. Appreciate those who appreciate you as well as those who despitefully use you. Put and keep on the whole armor of God so that you may walk the journey fully covered and equipped for whatever may come your way. Although things may come against you, and at times you may even trip and fall, know that it's not over until the end. Guard your heart, feed your mind and let nothing take away the knowing that this is your journey, and you can handle it.

KEEP WALKING!

Chapter Eight

Go Tell Your Story

It's time for a new beginning.
The number 8 biblically means new beginnings.

Life is filled with moments where you must take time to reset, start over or step into a new beginning. There is no clock that tells us when this time will come; rather, circumstances and situations become the compass for these life changing shifts.

` The circumstances and situations that you have been through, those things that have really moved your universe, have been the things, although challenging, that have given you a new perspective.

Things such as death, tragedy or even something you did that was shameful! Whatever the circumstances, your before perspective is greatly different than your after. These experiences have molded and shaped your life and given you a different perspective. Without it being spoken, all of those circumstances have created a new beginning in your life.

My hope for you!

It is my hope that after reading this book for 8 days, you will take the information and apply at least one of the lessons outlined, and then prepare yourself to share your story.

My own journey may be much like yours in that I have had to learn lessons, apply the information and share my message with someone else. As I reflect on my life, I realize that all of my many years of listening to Oprah played a part in preparing me for this moment in life. I realize that while I have had some tragic and life changing moments, it was not the end of the world. In fact, it gave me an opportunity to have a different conversation with God. A conversation that would afford me the chance to strengthen my belief in God and practice what I had been reading. The truth is my faith has been challenged at times. Even my conversations with the Creator have not always been those of understanding moments. However, at this point in my life my perspective was shifting me to a different place in my journey.

The Shift

The first thing that I had to do was jumpstart my healing process by forgiving myself. After years of forgiving other people and allowing myself to be vulnerable, I now had to take time to forgive John. I can honestly say, at that moment, I am not quite sure I knew what it meant to forgive myself, but I got there. I had to do what is sometimes a hard task for people, and that was to go back and remember all the advice that had been given to me. It was this process, and all my experiences that finally allowed me to understand what this phrase meant, "When the student is ready the teacher will appear." *It is now time for me to teach.*

As I stand in my ready position, it is my hope that you are standing in yours as well. It is time for you to go teach the universe. As you reflect on your journey, know that the circumstances of life only come to make you better. I know that sometimes it is difficult to see that in the moment when you are facing tragedy or a life altering moment, but it is simply the truth.

How do I really know?

Many times with the hustle and bustle of life and noise all around us, it is hard to hear what we need to move us to the next level. It is important that you are giving time and opening yourself up to the universe to speak to you. Listening not only gives you a much needed perspective, but also helps you to see that you become stronger and better through the lessons of life. You learn that life is so much more than material things and what is directly in front of you. In fact, life is not about the tangible, but the intangible.

Throughout your process you will hopefully learn a great deal. You will learn that when you have been chosen, and you have, that there is something inside of you, which I have coined; the ***"The Thing,"*** which will be my next book. That thing inside of you that has been perfected through the moments you may describe as crushing.

While you may not have understood the 'why' of your moments during the moment, I hope that today you have a different perspective and will take the challenge to share. Someone is waiting for your words of encouragement, your voice of wisdom and testimony to shift their life to their new beginning. They are waiting.

Don't be Silent

It is so important that you understand your voice, but not just any voice, one that will literally change lives. You may ask the question "Why Should I share? Will it really make a difference?" The answer is YES! Your voice makes a difference and what you share will impact lives. You will become a life giver through your words. Your words are powerful and will free people from bondage, give encouragement and help people out of dark places because you chose to share your experience. At the end of the day, it is a choice, your choice, and what you choose to do will not only affect you, but the lives of others as well. Your choice to share, if that's what you choose, could possibly be a life changing conversation that could give someone hope.

I encourage you today, go and tell your story. Tell it to whoever will listen. Share your truth and don't be ashamed of telling the truth and watch what will happen. Many may see things from one dimension, only what is going on from one view, when in actuality, there is always more than one thing going on at a time. You will find that as you share freely of yourself to help others, in the midst of this process, your healing process will also continue. You will find that you will gain more strength and knowledge through your sacrifice and that you are not the only one going through the process.

Many people have had dark encounters in their lives and they have learned to have a better life, but this knowledge has not come by sitting idle. It has not come by quieting their voice; it has come through sharing and empowering someone else. ***Go share*** your story with that family whose children were killed in a tragic accident, or shooting. ***Go share*** your story with that person who lost his/her parent, that person who was diagnosed with cancer, that person whose marriage may be destroyed. ***Go share*** your story! They are waiting to hear a testimony of victory, a journey of triumph and to see a living example of what it looks like to endure and win. They are waiting for a voice, and that voice is you. ***Go Share!***

Made in United States
Orlando, FL
09 January 2024